HYPE BRANDS

STÜSSY

KENNY ABDO

Fly!
An Imprint of Abdo Zoom
abdobooks.com

abdobooks.com

Published by Abdo Zoom, a division of ABDO, P.O. Box 398166, Minneapolis, Minnesota 55439. Copyright © 2023 by Abdo Consulting Group, Inc. International copyrights reserved in all countries. No part of this book may be reproduced in any form without written permission from the publisher. Fly!™ is a trademark and logo of Abdo Zoom.

Printed in the United States of America, North Mankato, Minnesota.
052022
092022

Photo Credits: Alamy, Getty Images, Shutterstock, ©Estevan Cruz p.10/ CC BY-NC-ND 2.0, ©Andrew Chee p.15/ CC BY-SA 2.0, ©Allen Lee p.16/ CC BY-NC-ND 2.0, ©Lawrence Butler p.18/ CC BY-NC 2.0
Production Contributors: Kenny Abdo, Jennie Forsberg, Grace Hansen
Design Contributors: Candice Keimig, Neil Klinepier, Laura Graphenteen

Library of Congress Control Number: 2021950289

Publisher's Cataloging-in-Publication Data

Names: Abdo, Kenny, author.
Title: Stüssy / by Kenny Abdo.
Description: Minneapolis, Minnesota : Abdo Zoom, 2023 | Series: Hype brands | Includes online resources and index.
Identifiers: ISBN 9781098228569 (lib. bdg.) | ISBN 9781644947999 (pbk.) | ISBN 9781098229405 (ebook) | ISBN 9781098229825 (Read-to-Me ebook)
Subjects: LCSH: Clothing and dress--Juvenile literature. | Brand name products--Juvenile literature. | Stüssy, Inc.--Juvenile literature. | Fashion--Social aspects-Juvenile literature. | Popular culture--Juvenile literature. | Surfing--Juvenile literature.
Classification: DDC 338.7--dc23

TABLE OF CONTENTS

Stüssy............................ 4

Hype............................. 8

All The Rage 14

Glossary 22

Online Resources 23

Index 24

STÜSSY

From a small surfboard shop to an entire fashion empire, Stüssy is a last name recognized around the world.

Beginning as one man's passion project, the brand grew into an unstoppable **streetwear** powerhouse.

HYPE

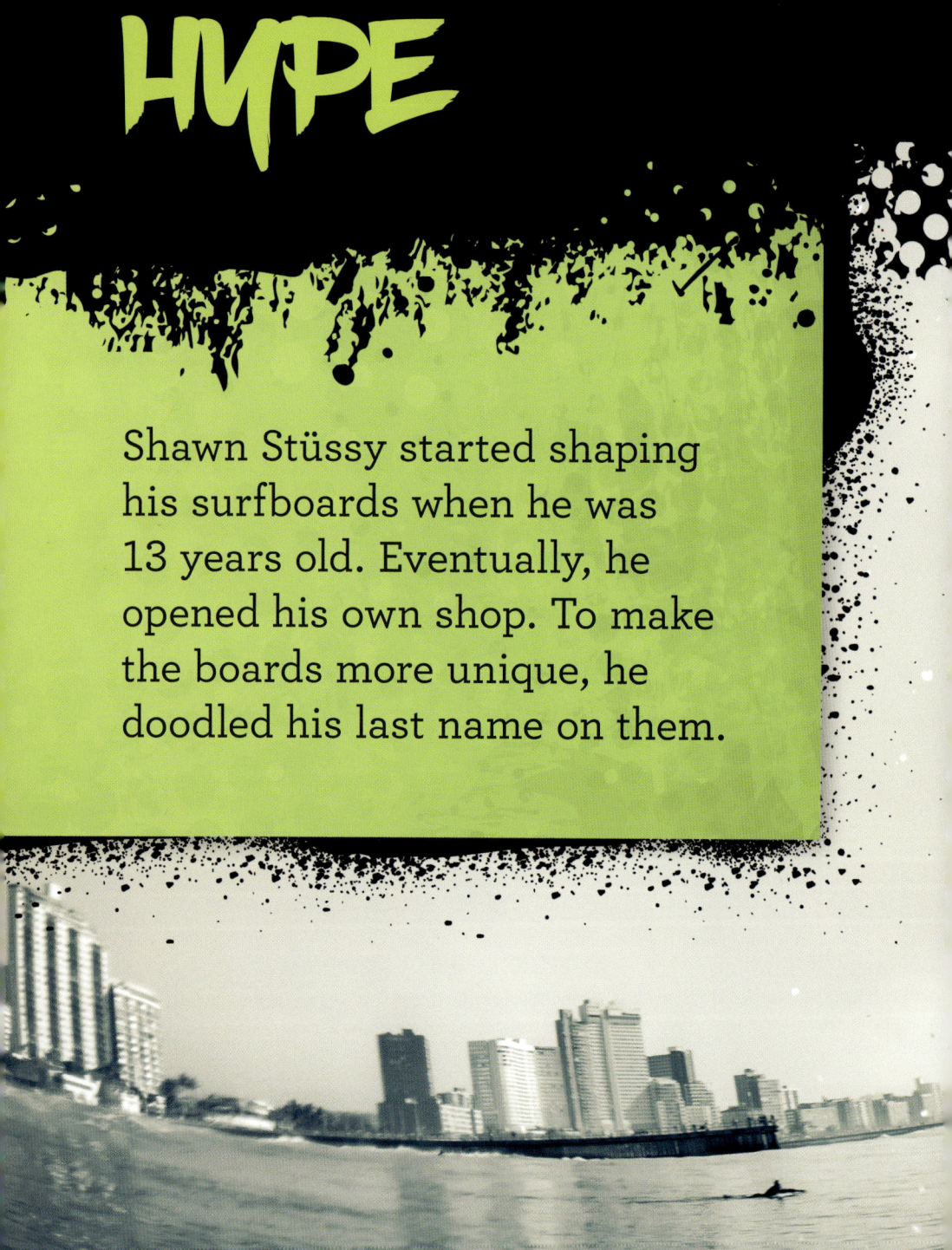

Shawn Stüssy started shaping his surfboards when he was 13 years old. Eventually, he opened his own shop. To make the boards more unique, he doodled his last name on them.

In the early '80s, Stüssy took black T-shirts and screen-printed his signature on them. By 1984, he had started an official clothing brand with his friend, Frank Sinatra Jr.

The line was an instant success around the world. In 1996, Stüssy resigned as president of the company. But the directions the brand could go from there were limitless.

ALL THE RAGE

In 1999, Stüssy sponsored a skateboarding team. The **roster** included skaters like Richard Mulder, Danny Montoya, and Keith Hufnagel. They helped build **cred** for the brand.

Stüssy and Nike first **collaborated** in 2000. The two **dropped** the popular Air Huarache. The team-up set the tone for how **streetwear** brands and sportswear labels could work together.

Stüssy celebrated 30 years of hype in 2010. The company released a collection with Supreme. In 2011, the brand worked with Marvel Comics to make limited-edition T-shirts!

Stüssy released a **capsule collection** in 2012. It was made up of custom varsity jackets for new members of the Stüssy Tribe, including famous rappers A$AP Rocky and Theophilus London.

In 2014, fans were thrilled when Stüssy **collaborated** with Vans to release a **throwback** collection of sneakers. In 2017, Stüssy opened a **flagship** store in Toronto where people could snag the hottest gear!

In 2020, Stüssy and Nike teamed up again after 20 years to release three celebrated sneaker **collaborations**. All of them sold out almost immediately.

Stüssy's signature has lasted the test of time. Without any alterations in decades, the logo has become the symbol of hype.

GLOSSARY

capsule collection – a smaller version of a designer's vision. Often it is with limited edition merchandise.

collaborate – to work with another person or group in order to do something or reach a goal.

cred – short for credibility. In pop culture, it refers to having popularity with the public, especially young people.

drop – when something that is highly anticipated is released to the public.

flagship – a brand's lead, largest, or most important store.

roster – a list of athletes on a team.

streetwear – fashionable, yet casual clothing worn by followers of popular culture. It is heavily influenced by hip-hop and surf culture.

throwback – when a product has the features of a past product.

ONLINE RESOURCES

Booklinks
NONFICTION NETWORK
FREE! ONLINE NONFICTION RESOURCES

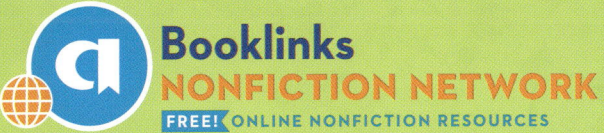

To learn more about Stüssy, please visit abdobooklinks.com or scan this QR code. These links are routinely monitored and updated to provide the most current information available.

INDEX

A$AP Rocky 17

Air Huarache 15

Canada 18

Hufnagel, Richard 14

logo 8, 10, 21

London, Theophilus 17

Marvel Comics 16

Montoya, Danny 14

Mulder, Richard 14

Nike (brand) 15, 20

Sinatra Jr., Frank 10

skateboarding 14

stores 8

Stüssy, Shawn 8, 10, 12

Supreme (brand) 16

surfing 5, 8

Vans (brand) 18